100% ONE DIRECTION: THE UNOFFICIAL BIOGRAPHY

A BANTAM BOOK  978 0 857 51069 3

First published in Great Britain by Bantam,
an imprint of Random House Children's Books
A Random House Group Company

Bantam edition published 2011

1 3 5 7 9 10 8 6 4 2

Text copyright © Bantam Books, 2011

Produced by Shubrook Bros. Creative
www.shubrookbros.com

Cover photos (L to R) © Paul Grover/Rex Features, © McPix Ltd/Rex Features, © Graham Stone/Rex Features, © Brian Rasic/Rex Features, © McPix Ltd/Rex Features, (BG) © Getty Images
Back cover photo ©McPix Ltd/Rex Features

P2-3 and p62-63: (all frames) © Getty images, © Graham Stone/Rex Features (x3), © Copetti/Photofab/MCP/Rex Features, © Beretta/Sims/Rex Features, © NTI Media Ltd/Rex Features, © McPix Ltd/Rex Features (x3), © Copetti/Photofab/Rex Features, © Gavin Rodgers/Rex Features, p4-5: (all) © McPix Ltd/Rex Features, p6-7 © David Fisher/Rex Features (for inserts see relevant pages), p8-9 (L) © Martin Karius/Rex Features, (TR) © Beretta/Sims/Rex Features, (BR) © Beretta/Sims/Rex Feature, p10-11 (TL) © Brian Rasic/Rex Features, (BL) © McPix Ltd/ Rex Features, (R) © McPix Ltd/Rex Features, p12-13 (BL) © Graham Stone/Rex Features, (TM) © McPix Ltd/Rex Features, (BM) © McPix Ltd/Rex Features, (R) © Jonathan Hordle/ Rex Feature, p14-15 (L) © Copetti/Photofab/MCP/Rex Features, (TM) © NTI Media Ltd/Rex Features, (BM) © Getty Images, (R) © Martin Karius/Rex Features, p16-17 (L) © McPix Ltd/ Rex Features, (TM) © Pawel Popek/Rex Features, (BM) © Startraks Photo/Rex Features, (R) © Graham Stone/Rex Features, p18-19 (L) © McPix Ltd/Rex Features, (TM) © Beretta/Sims/ Rex Features (BM) © McPix Ltd/Rex Features, (R) © Jonathan Hordle/Rex Features, p20-21 (L) © McPix Ltd/Rex Features, (TM) © Beretta/Sims/Rex Features, (BM) © Graham Stone/Rex Features, (R) © Graham Stone/Rex Features, p22-23 (L) © NTI Media Ltd/Rex Features, (R) © Copetti/Photofab/Rex Features, p24 © McPix Ltd/Rex Features (x2), p26-27 © Getty Images (x4), (TR) © Paul Grover/Rex Features, (MR) © Andrew G Hobbs/Getty Images, (BR) © McPix Ltd/Rex Features, p28-29 © Getty Images (x4), © istock, (TL) © Beretta/Sims/Rex Features, p30-31 (L) © Martin Karius/Rex Features, (BL) © Beretta/Sims/Rex Features, (TR) © McPix Ltd/Rex Features, (BM) © Graham Stone/Rex Features, (BR) © Copetti/Photofab/Rex Features, (TL circle) © istock, (BL circle) © Beretta/Sims/Rex Features, (TR circle) © Geoffrey Swaine/Rex Features, (BR circle) © David Fisher/Rex Features, p32-33 © McPix Ltd/Rex Features, p34-35 © Copetti/Photofab/Rex Features, p36-37 (L) © Copetti/Photofab/Rex Features, (ML) © Beretta/Sims/Rex Features, (MR) © Graham Stone/Rex Features, (R) © Beretta/Sims/Rex Features, p38-39 (L) © Beretta/Sims/Rex Features, (ML) © Martin Karius/ Rex Features, (MR) © McPix Ltd/Rex Features, (R) © Beretta/Sims/Rex Features, p40 (L) © McPix Ltd/Rex Features, (R) © Beretta/Sims/Rex Features, p42-43 © Brian Rasic/Rex Features , p44-45 © McPix Ltd/Rex Features, p46-47 (L) © NBCUPHOTOBANK/Rex Features, (circle images) © Paul Grover/Rex Features, (M) © Sipa Press/Rex Features, (TR) © Dezo Hoffmann/ Rex Features, (MR) © Startraks Photo/Rex Features, (BR) © Everett Collection/Rex Features, p48-49 © David Fisher/Rex Features, (BG) © Getty Images, p50-51 (TL) © NTI Media Ltd/Rex Features, (BL) © Getty Images, (R) © Brian Rasic/Rex Features, p52-53 (heart icon) © istock, (popcorn/ mayonnaise) © Getty images, (L to R) © McPix Ltd/Rex Features, © Beretta/Sims/ Rex Features, © Rex Features, © Beretta/Sims/Rex Features, © Brian Rasic/Rex Features, © Startraks Photo/Rex Features, © Rex Features, © McPix Ltd/Rex Features, © Beretta/Sims/Rex Features, p54-55 (M) © Beretta/Sims/Rex Features, (L top to bottom) © Graham Stone/Rex Features, © Copetti/Photofab/Rex Features, © Copetti/Photofab/Rex Features, © Beretta/Sims/Rex Features, © Beretta/Sims/Rex Features, p56-57 (L to R) © Rotello/MCP/ Rex Features, © Fiona Hamilton/Newspix/Rex Features, © David Fisher/Rex Features, © Copetti/Photofab/Rex Features, p58-59 (all) © McPix Ltd/Rex Features, p60-61 (L) © Rex Features, (TM) © Everett Collection/Rex Features, (BM) © Beretta/Sims/Rex Features, (R) © Picture Perfect/Rex Features. (Arrows throughout) © istock

Bantam Books are published by
Random House Children's Books,
61–63 Uxbridge Road, London W5 5SA

www.rbooks.co.uk

www.kidsatrandomhouse.co.uk

Addresses for companies within The Random House Group Limited can be found at:
www.randomhouse.co.uk/offices.htm

THE RANDOM HOUSE GROUP Limited Reg. No. 954009

A CIP catalogue record for this book is available from the British Library

Printed in China

THE 100% UNOFFICIAL BIOGRAPHY

# 100% ONE DIRECTION

EVIE PARKER

BANTAM
BOOKS

# 100% ONE DIRECTION
# CONTENTS

## What's inside?

8....... *The X Factor* Story
12..... 1D Profile: Harry
14..... 1D Profile: Louis
16..... 1D Profile: Liam
18..... 1D Profile: Zayn
20.... 1D Profile: Niall
22.... Simon Cowell: The Mentor
24.... Spot the Difference
25.... Crossword
26.... Which Direction?
28.... Favourite Things
30.... Practical Jokes
32.... Poster
34.... 10 Things to Love About 1D

### 1D PROFILE
### ZAYN

**The Basics**

Name..............Zayn Malik
Date of birth......January 12, 1993
Home Town.........Bradford
Star Sign..........Capricorn
Height............5' 9"
Eye colour........Brown
Hair colour........Black

LOVES

HATES Burping

Profiles from page: **12**

### 10 THINGS TO
### LOVE
### ABOUT 1D

There are thousands of things we love about One Direction, but we've managed to narrow it down to our top ten.

1 **Pranks**

2 **Hair**

3 **Ballads**

4 **Their Eyes**

5 **Cute Factor**

6 Love their

7 Their s

8 Fashio

9 Love fo

10 Am

Things to Love About 1D page: **34**

36.... 1D Style File: Harry

37..... 1D Style File: Louis

38.... 1D Style File: Liam

39.... 1D Style File: Zayn

40.... 1D Style File: Niall

41..... Word Search

42.... 1D Trivia

44 .... Boy Band Brains

46 .... Life Changing Influences

48.... Poster

50.... 1D Fan-Mania

52.... Perfect Dates

54.... 5 Become 1

56.... Judges' Verdicts

58.... Poster

60.... A-Z of 1D

Style File from page: **36**

Perfect Dates page: **52**

Boy Band Brains page: **44**

Poster page: **58**

# THE X FACTOR STORY

*From audition to stardom!*

Be prepared for 1D overload as we check out the amazing journey that shot Harry, Louis, Liam, Zayn and Niall to boy band stardom.

## The beginning

For these cute crooners, their amazing journey began when they auditioned in the first round of *The X Factor* as individual artists. These five boys were great. They showed heart, promise and vocal talent (not forgetting extremely good looks!) that immediately set them apart from the crowd, and each made it through to the next stage of the competition. They were on their way.

Then, the dreaded moment came. As the names were read out for Boot Camp, none of the boys were included. They assumed that their *X Factor* dreams were over and they prepared to pack their bags, put on their hoodies and head home. However, little did they know that Simon Cowell had other plans for the fresh-faced lads.

SUPERIOR

Five become one as Niall, Harry, Louis, Liam and Zayn become One Direction.

## The recall

Tension mounted as the boys were recalled to the stage. They were totally confused. They hadn't been put through to Boot Camp, and yet here they were, standing back in front of the judges, none of the boys knowing one another and none knowing why they were there. Then, the news came. They found out that they would be given the amazing opportunity to go to Boot Camp after all,

# These boys had heart, promise and vocal talent that would take them all the way.

but as a five piece boy band – a boy band with looks, strong vocals, amazing dance moves and mega pin-up appeal. Far from their dreams being over, they were just about to begin.

Niall, Zayn and Liam are now unable to walk the streets unnoticed.

# THE X FACTOR STORY

*From audition to stardom!*

## The Final

As *The X Factor* progressed, One Direction became stronger and more united every week. Belting out songs like 'My Life Would Suck Without You', 'The Way You Look Tonight' and 'Summer of '69' the boys cruised all the way to the final along with Matt Cardle, Rebecca Ferguson and Cher Lloyd. The heat was on and the competition was immense! For all of us, 1D were the hottest thing still in *The X Factor*, but their chance to win the competition and the million-pound recording contract was about to end. They followed Cher out of the competition after performing their version of 'Torn' and left thousands of us in tears. The guys were gone and the five reasons for tuning in on a Saturday and Sunday night were over. However, the boys with the X-appeal have not vanished. Since the final they have been on *The X Factor* Tour, bonding as a band and signed a recording contract with Simon Cowell's label. They went to LA to create their debut album and have had a list of producers lining up to work with them. It seems there's plenty more to come from our five favourite teen hotties. Hold onto your hearts everyone, hot is about to get much, much hotter!

Matt Cardle was great friends with the boys off stage.

## What's in a name?

One of the things we love about the boys is that they've all got their own traits. Zayn spends ages getting ready, Niall is the silly one in the group, Harry is the romantic and Liam and Louis have a mutual love for hair straighteners, but when Simon Cowell pulled them all together, they knew they had to work as a team and focus on one future. As they all wanted to move to the ultimate goal of pop superstardom, it was Harry who came up with the band name – One Direction.

## One Direction were the hottest thing in *The X Factor* and the cutest thing on TV!

## The X Factor Discography

| Week | Theme | Song | Artist |
|------|-------|------|--------|
| 1 | Number Ones | 'Viva La Vida' | Coldplay |
| 2 | Heroes | 'My Life Would Suck Without You' | Kelly Clarkson |
| 3 | Guilty Pleasures | 'Nobody Knows' | Pink |
| 4 | Halloween | 'Total Eclipse of the Heart' | Bonnie Tyler |
| 5 | American Anthems | 'Kids in America' | Kim Wilde |
| 6 | Elton John | 'The Way You Look Tonight' | Elton John |
| 7 | The Beatles | 'All You Need is Love' | The Beatles |
| 8 | Rock | 'Summer of '69' 'You Are So Beautiful' | Bryan Adams Joe Cocker |
| 9 | Club Classics | 'Only Girl in the World' 'Chasing Cars' | Rihanna Snow Patrol |
| 10 | The Final | 'Your Song' 'She's the One' 'Torn' | Elton John Robbie Williams Natalie Imbruglia |

# HARRY

## The Basics

Name ..................... Harry Styles
Date of birth ..... February 1, 1994
Home town ......... Holmes Chapel, Cheshire
Star Sign ............. Aquarius
Height ................... 5' 10"
Eye colour .......... Green
Hair colour .......... Brown

Harry started singing in a band called White Eskimo when he was 14 and two years later he auditioned for *The X Factor*. He immediately won Simon over. Louis Walsh was less convinced due to Harry's tender age, but Mr Styles went through to the next round to prove him wrong!

Harry is one of the most romantic members of 1D and wears his heart on his sleeve – and sometimes, that's all he wears! This curly-haired cutie likes to walk around stark naked and has even admitted to walking around The X Factor mansion in a gold thong!

These girl fans get a thumbs-up from Harry.

Harry Styles doing what he does best – singing and looking good!

**LOVES**
Giggling girls

**HATES**
Bad language

"Harry was charming. Louis didn't want him through... but he went through!
Simon Cowell

# 1D PROFILE
# LOUIS

## The Basics

Name ..................... Louis Tomlinson
Date of birth ..... December 24, 1991
Home town ......... Doncaster, South Yorkshire
Star Sign............. Capricorn
Height................... 5' 9"
Eye colour .......... Green/blue
Hair colour.......... Brown

Louis got three yesses when he first auditioned for *The X Factor* before ending up in One Direction. He's the messy one in the band and often leaves things dumped on the floor - much to the annoyance of the other boys. He's got a great sense of humour and loves to do silly voices and goof around. He hardly ever reads books but once tried reading David Beckham's Autobiography. He got halfway through before his dog ate the entire book... he took this as a sign and hasn't read since! Whilst only young, Louis had several jobs before ending up in 1D, including working at his local cinema and on a till at Doncaster Rovers Football Club!

Louis joking around outside *The X Factor* house in 2010.

### Did you know?

In an interview, Louis once joked that he likes 'girls who eat carrots'. Since then, girls have sent him carrots from across the whole country!

**LOVES**
Tanned girls

**HATES**
Tattoos

"It was the biggest stage he'd ever performed on – before that the biggest show he had done was Grease at Hall Cross School!"
Louis' mum

# LIAM

## The Basics

Name ..................... Liam Payne
Date of birth ..... August 29, 1993
Home town ......... Wolverhampton
Star Sign ............. Virgo
Height.................. 5' 10"
Eye colour ......... Brown
Hair colour......... Brown

**Did you know?**

Liam can play piano and guitar... but not at the same time!

Gorgeous Liam is the Justin Bieber look-a-like who loves his hair straighteners. He's a massive softy and a serious romantic, too. He takes pride in perfecting his hair and even claims that a certain Justin stole his style! He had already auditioned for *The X Factor* two years earlier when he was only 16. Simon Cowell loved him from the beginning, but poor Liam only made it as far as Judges' Houses before being sent home. This time he sang 'Cry Me a River' at his audition and blew the judges (and the rest of us) away. He's hot, cute, determined and seriously talented.

Liam strolls with his fans before posing for a picture.

Which hair came first – the Payne or the Bieber?

**LOVES**
Girls wearing
knee-high socks

**HATES**
Fake tans

**"** You've definitely
got it; whatever it
is, you've got it. **"**
Cheryl Cole

# 1D PROFILE
# ZAYN

## The Basics

Name ..................... Zayn Malik
Date of birth ..... January 12, 1993
Home town ......... Bradford
Star Sign ............. Capricorn
Height ................... 5' 9"
Eye colour .......... Brown
Hair colour .......... Black

Zayn loves being organized and has to know where all his gear is as the band travel around. He auditioned for *The X Factor* in Manchester where he gained three yesses from the judges. Problems arose for poor Zayn, though, when the contestants were forced to dance on stage for the first time. He refused to take part but Simon Cowell noticed he was missing and encouraged him on stage. We don't know what he was worried about - he's hiding some great moves!

Even on the move Zayn has time to throw a wave at his adoring fans.

You've got to hand it to him, Zayn loves his fans.

**LOVES**
Girls in high-
heeled shoes

**HATES**
Burping

I hadn't really
danced before
*The X Factor.*
Zayn

# 1D PROFILE
# NIALL

## The Basics

Name ..................... Niall Horan
Date of birth ..... December 13, 1993
Home town ......... Mullingar, Ireland
Star Sign ............. Virgo
Height ................. 5' 7"
Eye colour .......... Blue
Hair colour ......... Blond

Niall loves singing and dancing. In fact, he once said that his earliest childhood memory was singing. He first auditioned for *The X Factor* in Dublin where Louis Walsh famously said that people will warm to him because he's 'likeable'. We certainly agree, but it's Niall's talent and Irish charm that stole the show for us. Luckily, Katy Perry agreed and used her casting vote to push cheeky Niall through. He's shy around girls and puts this down to the fact he went to an all boys' school.

Niall trying to buy a paper without being noticed... no chance!

Niall and the boys prepare to greet their screaming fans.

Niall always takes time out to sign autographs for the 1D fans.

20

**LOVES**
Being funny

**HATES**
Cardigans

"I've been compared to
Justin Bieber a few times.
It's not a bad comparison."
Niall

21

# SIMON COWELL
# THE MENTOR

When this handsome fivesome was formed into a group, it was lucky Simon Cowell that got to mentor them throughout *The X Factor* – and later sign them to his record label, SyCo. Under Simon's guidance surely these boys can only be going in one direction! Superstardom here we come.

1D with Simon. What a proud mentor he is!

## On the up!

The boys loved having Simon as their mentor throughout *The X Factor* and now can't believe they're signed to his hugely successful record label. His experience and enthusiasm for One Direction's future are just what the boys needed to get them from third place on *The X Factor* to global stars!

The boys say that Simon is always on the phone giving his opinion and advice to bring them the ultimate success they desire. In fact, Simon was so confident in the potential success of these boys that it was rumoured he'd already brought on board songwriters and producers for the band's first album before the competition had even finished!

## Debut album

Simon Cowell is so trusting in 1D that he pretty much let them create the album they want to release. The boys always had a strong sense of the type of material they want to record and Simon has no doubt that they will follow in the likes of Take That, Westlife and JLS!

> **This is only the beginning for One Direction.**
> Simon Cowell

## 1D explosion!

Simon believes that 1D are about to explode onto the scene and totally stamp out the opposition. He checks in on the boys every now and then, but mainly to make sure everyone is working hard and that things are moving in the right direction. 1D wanted to surprise their fans with some of their song choices for the album. They worked with Steve Mac (the producer behind JLS) and loved every minute they were in the studio. Is Simon proud of his boys? You bet he is!

## Syco success

If Syco's past success is anything to go by, then the One Direction guys are in good hands. Previous artists to be signed to Simon's label include: Westlife, Leona Lewis, Alexandra Burke and Susan Boyle.

Simon knew the boys would be successful the moment he brought them together.

23

# SPOT THE DIFFERENCE

Can you spot the ten differences in the bottom picture of One Direction?

# CROSSWORD

You have to move in two directions to finish this crossword.
Check out the clues and see if you can get them right.

## ACROSS

1. *The X Factor* presenter
3. Zayn's home town
5. The blond-haired one
7. Cheryl's last name
8. Harry's star sign
10. Louis' favourite film
15. 1D's dueting partner in the final
16. Niall's star sign
17. Footy club where Louis worked

## DOWN

1. What Zayn doesn't like doing onstage
2. 1D's finishing place on *The X factor*
4. Aussie judge who loves 1D
6. He was second time lucky
9. _ _ _ _ Lloyd was a fellow competitor
11. Don't call me Mr Cowell
12. Liam likes girls in knee-high _ _ _ _ _
13. Justin _ _ _ _ _ _ who stole Liam's hair style
14. 1D's Judges' House song

# WHICH DIRECTION?

Want to be in the band? Follow the questions below to find out whether you could be the lucky sixth member of 1D or whether you'll be better backstage!

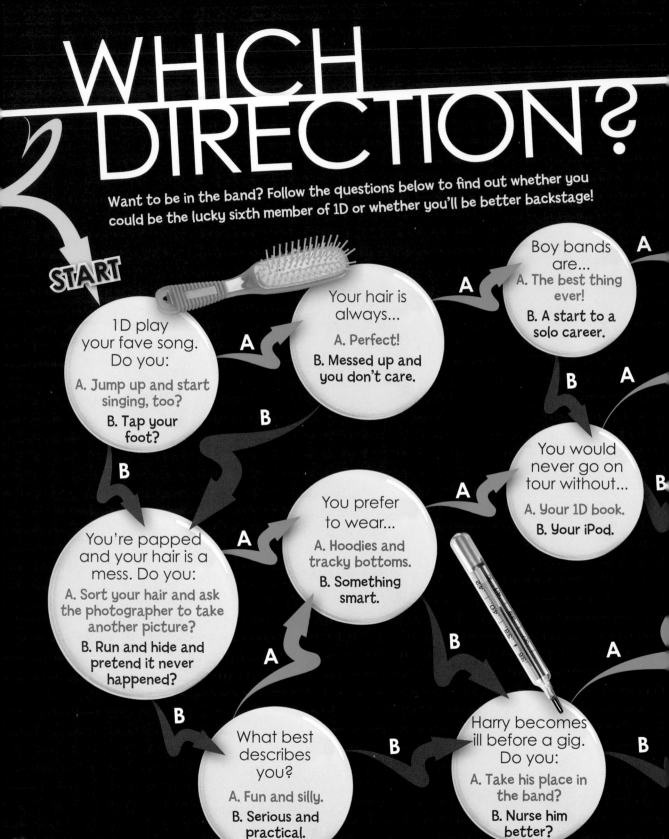

**START**

1D play your fave song. Do you:

A. Jump up and start singing, too?

B. Tap your foot?

Your hair is always...

A. Perfect!

B. Messed up and you don't care.

Boy bands are...

A. The best thing ever!

B. A start to a solo career.

You would never go on tour without...

A. Your 1D book.

B. Your iPod.

You're papped and your hair is a mess. Do you:

A. Sort your hair and ask the photographer to take another picture?

B. Run and hide and pretend it never happened?

You prefer to wear...

A. Hoodies and tracky bottoms.

B. Something smart.

What best describes you?

A. Fun and silly.

B. Serious and practical.

Harry becomes ill before a gig. Do you:

A. Take his place in the band?

B. Nurse him better?

## You're in One Direction

Congrats! You could perform in One Direction. You'd be a great addition to the band and might even get lead vocals! Woop, woop!

## You're behind the boys

You did well at your 1D audition, but you're not quite ready to take centre stage. You would be hired as a fantastic backing dancer though! Get up close and personal!

## Number one fan

You're not cut out for joining One Direction on stage just yet. However, you are a number one fan, so get out your banner and follow these boys wherever they go!

If you went on *The X Factor* you would get...

A. Three yesses.
B. A split decision.

A

A

B

B

Do you prefer to:
A. Write songs?
B. Dance around?

A

The tour bus breaks down. Do you:

A. Give everyone a piggyback to the show?
B. Chill and wait for help?

A

B

B

A

Your friends would say you're:

A. Out-going and a great singer.
B. Shy and quite quiet.

B

Your microphone breaks. Do you:

A. Just sing louder?
B. Run off stage?

# FAVOURITE THINGS

The 1D boys love everything from films to fashion and hair to hot pants, so let's delve into their secret box and see what these boys really adore!

## Knee Socks

Liam has a thing for knee socks... on girls of course, not for himself!

## Pussy Cats

His hair might look like a mane, but curly locks Harry, has a soft spot for cats.

## Hoodies

All the boys have one as it's easy to throw on for that casual but cool look.

There's no doubt that 1D are at the top of our favourite list! Let's take a look at some more of their fave things...

**Harry**
Fave colour: Blue
Fave film: *Love Actually*
Fave band: The Beatles
Fave man crush: Louis Tomlinson

**Liam**
Fave colour: Purple
Fave film: *Toy Story*
Fave singer: Michael Bublé
Fave man crush: Michael McIntyre

**Zayn**
Fave colour: Blue
Fave TV show: *The Simpsons*
Fave singer: Mario
Fave man crush: Justin Timberlake

**Louis**
Fave colour: Dark red
Fave film: *Grease*
Fave band: The Fray
Fave man crush: Robbie Williams

**Niall**
Fave colour: Green
Fave film: *Grease*
Fave singer: Beyoncé
Fave man crush: Michael Bublé

# Hair Straighteners

Liam's not the only one to own a pair, but apparently his straighteners are pink so he gets a special mention here!

# Hot Pants

Niall loves gold hot pants. Do we detect a fan of Kylie's 'Spinning Around' video here?

# Brunettes

Zayn has a thing for brown-haired girls. That might explain why he and Geneva Lane were an item.

# Dark Glasses

Louis wore them while presenting *The X Factor* Megamind competition and he can't get enough of them.

# PRACTICAL JOKES

We all know that One Direction are a bit cheeky, but did you know that they don't just play practical jokes on one another? There are many unsuspecting victims of the 1D boys' pranks. Let's take a look...

## Boxed in!

### Victim: Paparazzi

While waiting outside a recording studio during *The X Factor*, a group of photographers noticed that Harry was missing from the band. All the other four boys were there and it immediately sparked whispers that Harry had left 1D. However, seconds later Harry burst out of a box that he had been hiding in all along. He shot Styrofoam everywhere and sent the gathered media into hysterics. Brilliant!

## Stolen underwear

### Victim: Belle Amie

During an evening in *The X Factor* house, Harry was reported to have stolen a bra from one of the Belle Amie girls. This in itself is pretty bad, but was made even worse when Harry decided to put it on his head and go running around the house. Curly locks just never stops!

Belle Amie and the boys became great friends during *The X Factor*.

# We've got your number!

## Victim: Matt Cardle

The naughty two of 1D, Harry and Louis, love getting up to mischief when there are unsuspecting victims around – this time the victim was unlucky Matt Cardle. The boys were in the middle of a live chat on Twitter when they 'accidentally' let Matt's mobile number slip. Poor Matt woke the next morning to find thousands of missed calls and messages on his phone. Let's hope that one of those was an apology from Harry and Louis! Naughty!

Harry and Louis up to their old tricks!

The other half of Larry Stylenson!

## Anyone seen Louis?

## Victim: Simon Cowell

One night during the shooting of *The X Factor*, Louis decided to pull a prank on Simon Cowell and *The X Factor* crew and just ran away! Whether he fancied a night off or had an errand to run we don't quite know, but he almost gave Simon a heart attack. Apparently, Louis said he would be back soon, but he never returned!

100% ONE DIRECTION

# 10 THINGS TO LOVE ABOUT 1D

There are thousands of things we love about One Direction, but we've managed to narrow it down to our top ten.

## 1 Pranks
Harry and Louis are the main pranksters, but they all get in on the action once in a while.

## 2 Hair
Oh, the hair! Short, curly or long... We love all their locks!

## 3 Ballads
Those power ballads the boys knocked out on *The X Factor* had us eating out the palm of their hands.

## 4 Their Eyes
Green, brown or blue we don't care what colour they are, we just know how they make us feel when they look at us! Swoon!

## 5 Cute Factor
Want five boys with the cute factor? Look no further...

## 6 Love their mums

These boys are growing up fast, but we love the way they're still down to earth and love their mums.

## 7 Their smiles

Their gorgeous pearly-whites look like they've had the trademark Cowell-treatment.

## 8 Fashion

From suits to hoodies, 1D can make any outfit look hot. We're even sold on those strange jumpsuits... well, almost.

## 9 Love for their fans

1D appreciate their fans so much and always have time for them. They love us and we love them right back.

## 10 Amazing voices

Their voices can go from sweet to powerful in a second and can charm us or knock us off our feet. We love you 1D!

# HARRY

## Look 1

Harry's style is all about feeling good. He's always up for comfortable, casual clothing that is easy to throw on. His key styles are untucked shirts, loose jumpers and the hoodie but none would be complete without that classic Harry hairdo!

**STYLE TIP**

Grow your hair, chuck stuff on and just feel good.

Curly locks

Baggy hoodie

Colourful watch

## Look 2

For this look Harry sticks with boots but this time goes for a workman-style. These boots go great with military trousers and a relaxed shirt. Harry adds some bracelets and keeps the shirt untucked for that comfortable look. Thumbs up to you, too, Harry!

Grey jogging bottoms

Trainer boots

# 1D STYLE FILE
# LOUIS

*Swept hair*

## Look 1

Louis is a fan of summer fashion as it's the time of year when he can rock out in his favourite items. He loves everything from hoodies to cardies, but could never get by without his classic rolled up trousers and funky summer shoes.

### STYLE TIP

For that laid-back summer look go for espadrilles and rolled up trousers.

*Polo shirt*

*Denim roll ups*

## Look 2

On those colder days, Louis wraps up with a body-warmer and hat. He keeps things casual with loose fitting jogging bottoms but no matter what the weather, Louis rocks his espadrilles!

*Espadrilles*

# LIAM

Bieber hair style

## Look 1

Liam keeps his style cool and simple, often choosing to wear a plain or printed T-shirt with jeans. He adds some accessories — big belts, leather wristbands — to complete the look and teams with jackets and hoodies. He makes urban styling look easy!

**STYLE TIP**

*You can never go wrong with a plain white T-shirt.*

Printed T-shirt

Leather belt and wristbands

Dark jeans

## Look 2

Liam manages to pull off smart-casual perfectly. He simply loses the T-shirt and replaces it with a fashion-forward checked shirt. This keeps Liam feeling comfortable and also warmer on those chilly days.

Workman boots

# ZAYN

## Look 1

Zayn *loves* his clothes and spends time getting ready every morning – even though he makes it look like he's just thrown his outfit together. He loves his hoodies and even teams them with smart jackets.

## STYLE TIP

Never try too hard when creating your style. Just make it look effortless.

Necklace

Hoodie

Tracky bottoms

Colourful trainers

## Look 2

Zayn often keeps with the same style of T-Shirt and hoodie, but sometimes he alters his hair to change the look. Here he brushes his hair down instead of spiking it up. Subtle difference, but both work for us!

# NIALL

Scruffy hair

## Look 1

There's no denying that Niall loves having fun and he lets his clothes in on the action too. He often wears multi-coloured watches and wristbands to funk up his outfits. Whatever style Niall goes for, it always looks great with those cute blond locks on top.

### STYLE TIP

Wearing bracelets and watches can really snazzy-up any outfit.

Long-sleeved T-shirt

Colourful wristbands

Crunched-up jeans

## Look 2

Niall loves his body-warmers, so when the weather allows, it's the first thing in the wardrobe that he goes for. He also swaps the long-sleeved top for a zip-up. Perfect for popping up that hood to help escape the gaze of his waiting fans.

White trainers

# WORD SEARCH

Take a peek at the word search below and see if you can find the hidden One Direction-related words.

CHERYL   HARRY   X FACTOR
CUTE  LIAM  SYCO  ZAYN  HAIR
LOUIS  COWELL  NIALL  FAME

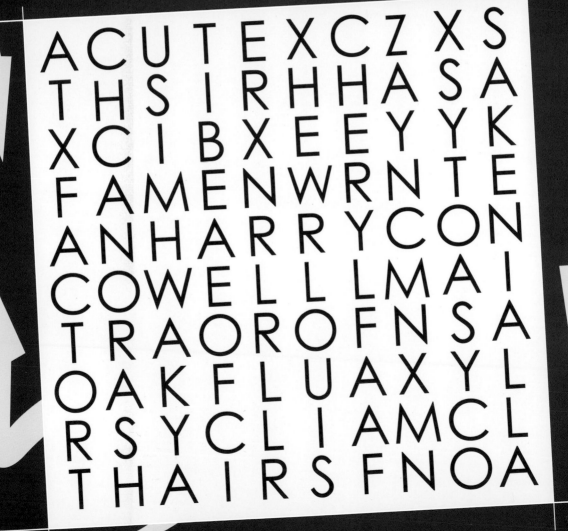

```
A C U T E X C Z X S
T H S I R H H A S A
X C I B X E E Y Y K
F A M E N W R N T E
A N H A R R Y C O N
C O W E L L L M A I
T R A O R O F N S A
O A K F L U A X Y L
R S Y C L I A M C L
T H A I R S F N O A
```

# ONE DIRECTION
# TRIVIA

Are you One Direction's number one fan? There's only one way to find out – put your pen to paper and see how you rate on this trivia test.

**1** Who is the oldest member of the band?

A. Liam
B. Louis
C. Harry

**2** Who got through to Boot Camp on *The X Factor* in 2008?

A. Harry
B. Liam
C. Niall

**3** Harry was in a band before One Direction. What was it called?

A. White Eskimo
B. Red Fireballs
C. Blue Whale

**4** What is Louis' favourite film?

A. *Transformers*
B. *Grease*
C. *High School Musical*

**5** Who initially refused to dance at Boot Camp?

A. Zayn
B. Harry
C. Liam

**6** Which member is from Ireland?

A. Harry
B. Niall
C. Louis

**7** Niall doesn't like...

A. Watches
B. Trainers
C. Cardigans

**8** When is Harry's birthday?

A. February 1
B. May 5
C. December 7

**9** Who went out with Geneva Lane?

A. Liam
B. Zayn
C. Louis

**10** Who has the star sign Aquarius?

A. Liam
B. Harry
C. Zayn

43

# BOY BAND BRAINS

## Perfect Hair

To some of us, perfect hair is a dream... something we will never achieve. For 1D, perfect hair comes naturally (well, kind of!). Whether it's Harry's curls, Louis and Liam's Bieber-look, or Zayn and Niall's finely tuned barnets, these boys just need a mirror, a hairdryer and some straighteners and they're away.

## The Look!

When the hair, the smouldering eyes and the outfits all come together, the 1D look takes care of itself. But the boys never want to leave anything to chance, so they spend a fair chunk of their day thinking about their clothes. Careful attention must be taken to make sure that the look is right for all occasions!

## Vocals

Vocals are the area of the brain that 1D have to focus on least. From their *X Factor* auditions to their debut album, these boys know how to belt out a tune. Their voices are already pitched perfectly, so a bit of vocal coaching here and there and they're ready to perform.

What does your favourite boy band think about? Ever wanted to get inside their heads? Well, here's your chance to unscramble those beautiful brains.

## Girl Fans

Where would a great boy band be without their adoring fans? We love them individually and as a group and no one appreciates this more than the boys themselves. These grateful lads will do all they can to sign autographs and have their pictures taken. This is a crucial part of who 1D are and they spend a fair chunk of the day thinking about their fanbase.

## Slow-Mo Video Poses

Like all good boy bands, our 1D boys spend hours thinking about how to create that slow-motion look for their music videos. It's all in the half-closed eyes, cute pout and slow head turn. This is vital to the success of any boy band, so the 1D hotties spend loads of time thinking about how to perfect it.

### Did you know?

Louis once thought about becoming a professional footballer. He has no time to think about that now, though, as it's music on the brain 24/7!

# LIFE CHANGING INFLUENCES

What would happen if the boys followed in the same paths as their idols and took their look to the ultimate extreme? We delve into our crystal ball to see how they would end up.

## Harry

### Elvis Presley

Harry's ultimate idol is Elvis Presley, but swapping that soft, curly hair for a quiff and a Vegas jumpsuit could be a big mistake! Although Hazza has been spotted in a jumpsuit of his own! Look out guys, the King has left the building!

## Liam

### Usher

Following in Usher's finely-tuned footsteps would mean that Liam would have to shave his gorgeous locks off. Not only that, but he would have to mentor Justin Bieber... the guy he claims stole his hair style in the first place!

Not even Harry manages to pull-off the Elvis jumpsuit.

## Niall

# Frank Sinatra

Niall loves the coolness of Frank Sinatra. Sinatra had the nickname 'Ol' Blue Eyes', so at least Niall doesn't have to change anything there. He's already got the cheeky smile, too, so all he needs is a hat to complete that Sinatra look.

Ol' Blue Eyes himself.

## Zayn

# Justin Timberlake

We'd say that Zayn has loads of the coolness and charm of JT, so he's closer than he realizes to his pop idol. All he needs are some super-slick dance moves and he'll be laughing!

JT pulling off the glasses look.

## Louis

# Danny Zuko

Louis loves the film, Grease. If his idol was someone like Danny Zuko then he'd have to abandon those polo shirts and rolled up trousers and get into that leather jacket! Put some grease in your hair and you're ready to go, Louis!

John Travolta as Danny Zuko.

One of Liam's many idols – Usher.

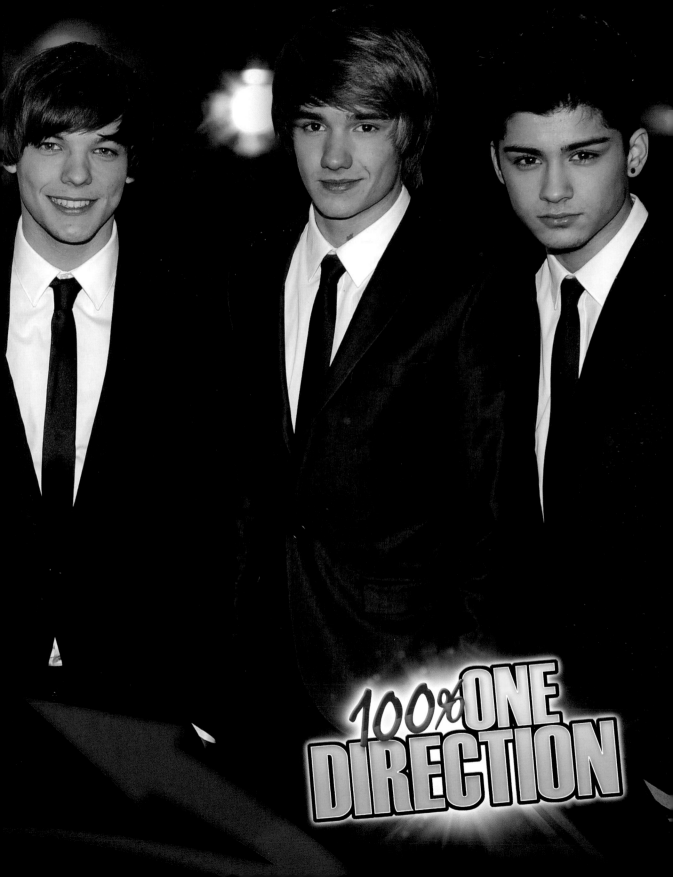

100% ONE DIRECTION

# 1D-MANIA!

You may love One Direction more than Cowell loves himself, but it's time to check out some of the mad and outrageous things 1D fans have got up to around the world.

## Police rescue

After recording their debut album in LA, the boys planned a secret return to the UK. However, word got out and as they arrived at Heathrow airport, 1D were mobbed by over 100 fans! Things got so crazy that they eventually had to be rescued by the police and whisked to safety.

Fans old and young go crazy for One Direction!

## We love you One Direction!
Screaming fan

## Staying grounded

During *The X Factor*, Harry got into some trouble with his fans. He was stepping out of a cab as he arrived to rehearse dance moves for a Saturday night show when he was suddenly engulfed by screaming girls who wanted to hug the 1D cutie. But it all went a bit wrong as Harry was pulled to the ground and had to be rescued by band-mate Liam!

## Mum Direction

One Direction have no bigger fans on the planet than their mums. When these boys were hotting up the stage during the show, their mums were behind them all the way – screaming, shouting and making sure that everyone voted for their brilliant boys!

> **I feel incredibly proud and it's all so surreal to see my boy on the stage.**
> Harry's mum

## Toe signing

Some of the 1D fans take their obsession a bit too far. The boys once revealed that they have been asked to sign some pretty weird stuff – the weirdest being someone's big toenail!

## Twitter race

In a race to secure the most followers on Twitter, Liam comes out on top. Poor Louis comes in last, with Harry second, Zayn third and Niall in fourth place. Tweet on boys... tweet on!

## Liam Bieber

Last winter Liam found himself being chased through the streets of LA by a crowd of screaming girls. The band were shocked that they were instantly so popular across the pond. However, their excitement turned to hysterical laughter as they realized why Liam was being chased... the girls thought he was Justin Bieber!

> **Think I need to change my look!**
> Liam on the Bieber chase

# PERFECT
# DATES

Ever dreamed of a date with your favourite 1D boy? Well, just in case you strike it lucky, here are a few handy hints on what to expect.

## Harry keeps it simple

Harry loves nothing more than a movie and popcorn on a date. As he's a true romantic, he would take you to see one of his favourite films, *Love Actually*. Make sure he doesn't fall asleep during the movie though. By his own admission, Harry is a very loud snorer! Harry's always great fun on a date and his ideal date would be with Cheryl Cole.

## Louis in love

Louis is a classic comedy film fan so he would probably take you to see his favourite movie, *Grease*. As he's got an awesome singing voice, he might take you to a singalong version, too. So get practising your Sandy lines! He loves girls with sweet voices and his top date would be with Diana Vickers.

## Liam the kid

Liam is a hopeless romantic, so you're bound to have a great time with him. A candlelit dinner for two, perhaps? A picnic in the park? Or maybe a show in the West End – he's going to pull out all the stops to make sure you have the perfect evening. But don't bring up his secret crush Leona Lewis – or he'll spend the date talking about her. Move on, Leona!

## Zayn insane

Zayn loves eating out so he'd probably take you to a fancy restaurant. Having said that, he spent his 18th birthday at Nandos, so don't get your hopes up! He has a crush on Megan Fox and doesn't like punks. So, if you're a girl who loves nose rings and Mohican hairstyles, you'd better change your style first.

## No way, Niall

Niall is a big joker so if you're after a sensible, romantic evening out then you've picked the wrong 1D boy. If Niall does take you on a date, it might be best not to go for a meal. Niall has a major phobia of mayonnaise and once said that he'd rather lick another man's armpit than eat the stuff. Nice Niall... really classy!

Mayonnaise

# FIVE BECOME ONE

Think of your top five boys – Harry, Louis, Liam, Zayn and Niall, right? Well, ever wondered what the hottest boy in the world would look like? Here we can show you for the very first time as our five dream boys become a super hot 1D ultraboy!

## FACE FACTS

Harry's hair

**Did you know?**
Harry's hair hasn't always been like this – when he was younger it used to be straight and blond!

Zayn's eyes

Niall's nose

Louis's mouth

Liam's jaw line

# ULTIMATE STYLE

## Liams's Cap
Going for that cool US vibe with the back-to-front baseball cap.

## Zayn's Hoodie
Tight-fitting hoodies mean that those defined muscles don't get lost in the look.

## Harry's man-bag
Forget backpacks – the way to carry things now is with a vintage man-bag as Harry often demonstrates.

## Louis' trousers
Show off those shins with Louis' classic roll-ups.

### Did you know?
The boys each own a romper suit with a zip-up hood! This means we can't tell who's who and they have no idea either!

## Niall's trainers
Colourful and comfortable. Niall's trainers do the trick.

# JUDGES' VERDICTS

The 1D boys were always a firm favourite with *The X Factor* judges who know how to spot the next big thing. Let's take a look at some of the comments they gave to the boys throughout the show.

## Louis Walsh

"I've never seen a band cause so much hysteria, so early in their career!"

"You proved tonight you're not just another boy band, you're a brilliant, brilliant vocal group."

"You're potentially the next big boy band."

## Dannii Minogue

"You are a boy band doing exactly what a boy band should do!"

"You're five heart-throbs."

## Cheryl Cole

# "You're my guilty pleasure!"

"You have all the right ingredients!"

"I can't even cope with how cute you are. Seriously! I just want to go up and hug them... in a nice way."

## Simon Cowell

# "I am as proud of you as people as I am as artists"

"You're 17, you don't believe the hype, you work hard, you rehearse... It's a total pleasure working with you."

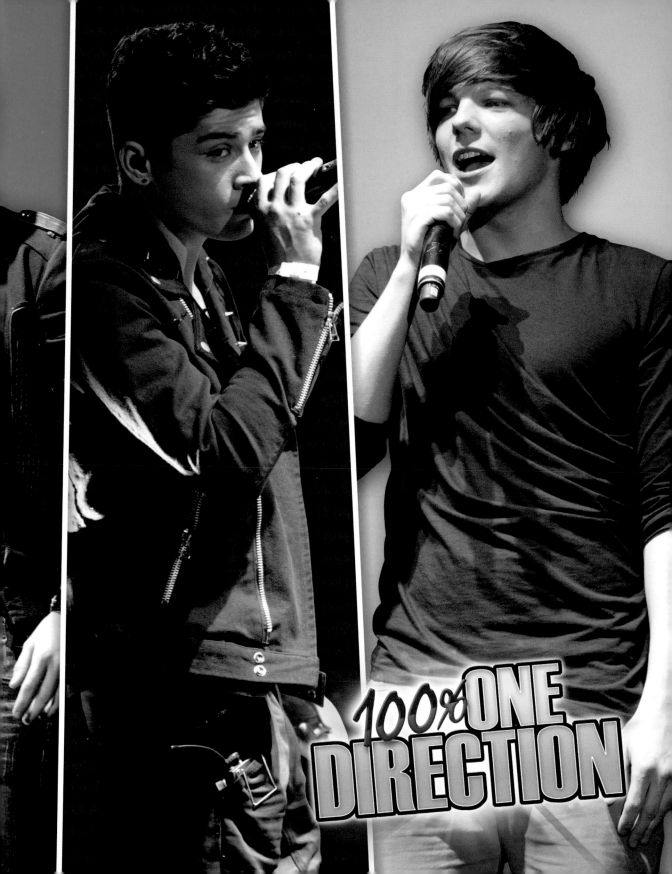

100% **ONE DIRECTION**

# THE ULTIMATE A-Z OF ONE DIRECTION

Take a trip through the alphabet in 1D style. A-Z never looked so good.

*Grease* is Niall and Louis' top film ever!

The X Factor presenter Dermot O'Leary.

'H' is for hair, but could also be for Harry-in-a-hat!

| | |
|---|---|
| **A** | **Auditions** – The stepping stone to *The X Factor* success |
| **B** | **Boot Camp** – Boys sing 'Torn' and rock to the finals |
| **C** | **Cheryl** – 1D are so cute, she just wants to hug them |
| **D** | **Dermot** – The presenter who introduced us to 1D |
| **E** | **Eldest** – Louis's the daddy of the band |
| **F** | **Fans** – The boys wouldn't be where they are without them |
| **G** | **Grease** – Louis and Niall's favourite movie |
| **H** | **Hair** – All five of them have super-sleek dos! |
| **I** | **Inspiration** – The boys have loads, from Elvis to Usher |
| **J** | **Jokes** – Watch out, these boys are big jokers |
| **K** | **Karaoke** – Liam used to go to impress the girls |
| **L** | **Liam** – Second time lucky for this boy |
| **M** | **Miming** – The boys don't believe in it and don't do it |
| **N** | **Niall** – Blond, cute and loaded with Irish charm! |
| **O** | **One Direction** – Best. Band. Ever. |
| **P** | **Paparazzi** – Smile boys, you're on the front page |
| **Q** | **Quids in** – These boys certainly won't be short of cash |
| **R** | **Robbie** – 1D's smouldering duet partner |
| **S** | **Style** – Whatever the look, these boys have it! |
| **T** | **Tomlinson** – Louis' pranks keeps us all in stitches! |
| **U** | **Underwear** – Harry once wore a gold thong! |
| **V** | **Virgo** – Niall's star sign |
| **W** | **Wolverhampton** – Where Liam was born |
| **X** | **The X Factor** – The springboard for pop superstardom |
| **Y** | **Yvie Burnett** – A vocal coach on *The X Factor* |
| **Z** | **Zayn** – Takes ages to get ready - but always looks great! |

Robbie sang his hit, 'She's the One' with 1D.

# Answers

PAGE 24

PAGE 25

DERMOT  BRADFORD
DANI
COLE  HALL
RED  IN
AQUARIUS
SREASE  I
CHE
ROBBIE  S  VIRGON
M  SOCK  BIEBER  TORN
O  R
DONCASTER

PAGE 41

PAGE 42

ACUTEXCZXS
THSTRHHASA
XCIBXEEYYK
FAMEINWRNTE
ANHARRIYCON
COWELILLMAII
TTRAOROFNSA
OAKFLUAXYL
RSYCLIIAMCL
THATRSFNOA

1 - B    6 - B
2 - B    7 - C
3 - A    8 - A
4 - B    9 - B
5 - A    10 - B

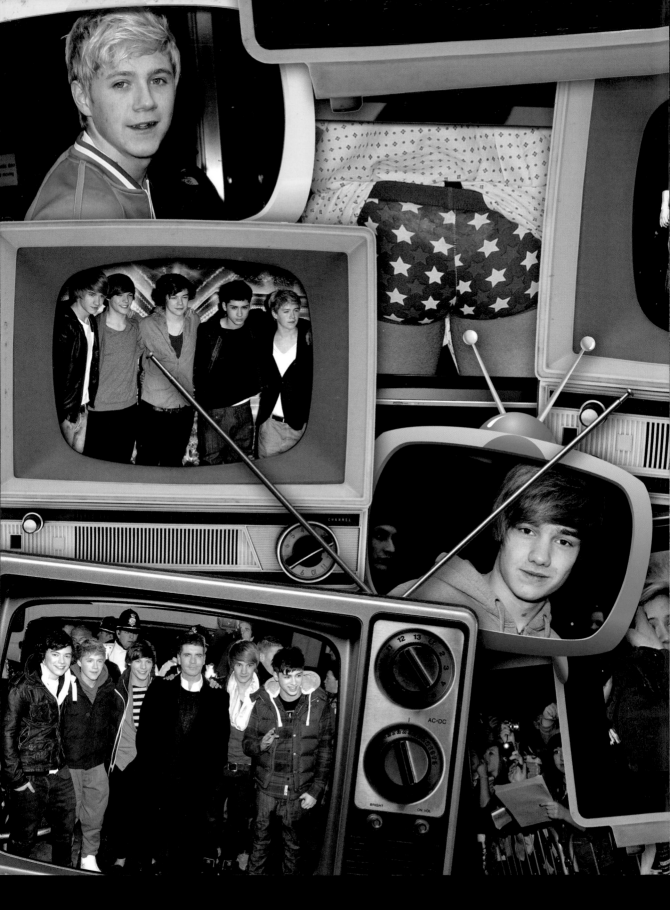